The REBUS Book

The REBUS Book

PICTURE PUZZLES

Martin Greif

Sterling Publishing Co., Inc.   New York
A STERLING/MAIN STREET BOOK

Library of Congress Cataloging-in-Publication Data

Greif, Martin, 1938-
    The rebus book : picture puzzles to tax your mind / Martin Greif
        p.   cm.
    "A Sterling/Main Street book."
    Includes index.
    ISBN 0-8069-3826-9
    1. Rebuses.   I. Title
    PN6371.G75 1996
    793.73—dc20   95-21955
                                                          CIP

10 9 8 7 6 5 4 3 2 1

A Sterling/Main Street Book

Published by Sterling Publishing Company, Inc.
387 Park Avenue South, New York, N.Y. 10016
© 1996 by Sterling Publishing Company, Inc.
Distributed in Canada by Sterling Publishing
C/o Canadian Manda Group, One Atlantic Avenue, Suite 105
Toronto, Ontario, Canada M6K 3E7
Distributed in Great Britain and Europe by Cassell PLC
Wellington House, 125 Strand, London WC2R 0BB, England
Distributed in Australia by Capricorn Link (Australia) Pty Ltd.
P.O. Box 6651, Baulkham Hills, Business Centre, NSW 2153, Australia
Manufactured in the United States of America
All rights reserved

ISBN 0-8069-3826-9

CONTENTS

That which is sensible more forcibly strikes
the memory than that which is intellectual.

—Francis Bacon

The rebus is a representation by means of pictures, letters, or figures of some word, phrase, or sentence. In its origin it dates back to
the beginning of written language, for the Chinese and Egyptian
writings are composed of images, and the records of ancient tombs
may be looked upon as a series of rebuses. Just as primitive efforts
in speech needed a great deal of accompanying gesture, so early
writings required images for adequate definite expressions of ideas.
There is this difference, however, between Chinese and Egyptian
picture-writing and the medieval, nineteenth-century, and modern
rebus—namely, that whereas in the former the intention is simplifi-
cation, in the latter two it is mostly mystification.

The ancient Greeks made frequent use of the rebus on the coins
of their cities and islands. Thus the Greek colony of Selinus, in
Sicily, which derived its name from the wild parsley growing there
in profusion, was represented on its coins by an image of this plant.
In the same way the coins of Rhodes bore a rose, those of Melos a

9

pomegranate, those of Phocaea a seal, and the city of Ancona was represented by a bent arm, the city's name derived from the Greek word meaning a bend. These have been termed *types parlants*, or

canting devices. Two Greek architects are said to have carved on their buildings the images of a frog and a lizard, these two words in Greek being respectively identical with their names, which they were forbidden to inscribe in written language.

Julius Caesar, according to Addison, used the image of an elephant on his coins because his name happened in the Punic language to stand for that animal. This is doubtful, however, as the elephant was commonly used as an emblem on coins. There are, nevertheless, undoubted examples of the use of the rebus on Roman coins, as, for example, those of Quintus Voconius *Vitulus*, on which a calf is represented, and those of L. Aquillius *Florus*, of which the following is an example:

It is in Picardy that the rebus more especially has flourished in the past. Sieur des Accords says that the rebus was a special product of that district, just as bayonets were associated with Bayonne, and mustard with Dijon. The people of Picardy were so much pleased with this kind of wit that their use of it became almost a madness, and if all their work of this kind could have been collected it would have been enough, in the language of Des Accords, "to load ten mules." He was judged of no account who did not take part in this kind of exercise. In the time of Edward III the English began to admire these "foreign fooleries in painted Poesie," as William Camden wrote in the sixteenth century, and "they which lacked wit to express their conceit in speech, did use to depaint it out (as it were) in pictures which they call *Rebus* by a Latine name well fitting their device. These were so liked by our English there, and sent over the streght of Calice, with full sail, were so entertained here (although they were most ridiculous) by all degrees, by the learned and unlearned, that he was no body that could not hammer out of his name an invention by this wit-craft, and picture it accordingly: whereupon who did not busie his brain to hammer this device out of his forge?"

Some French authorities have supposed that the word "rebus" originated from the custom followed by the clerks of the Basoche of making every year in the time of the Carnival a number of lampoons, which were entitled *De rebus quae geruntur*," or "Concerning things which are happening." These were read by the clerks, who were drawn through the streets in a cart. According to Ménage, this custom lasted at Boulogne till about 1630, when it was stopped by the police. The word "rebus" is accounted for as being a survival of this title, *De rebus quae geruntur*, the popular mind being able only to remember a portion of the expression. But it is simpler and probably more correct to understand the word as indicating the representation of ideas "by things."

Certain coins found in the neighborhood of Amiens reveal rebuses very complicated and impossible to translate with any certainty. These coins, made of lead, were distributed at the burlesque Feasts of Fools and Feasts of Innocents. The enormous number of them is evidence of the popularity of the rebus in this district. Where possible, French towns, like those of ancient Greece, have adopted some punning representation. Thus Arras is imaged by rats, three of which animals may be seen running round the coins of the city. It was said in a kind of proverb that the French would take Arras when the rats ate the cats. Lyons would obviously be represented by a lion. The treatment of Dijon is less obvious, its rebus being "dix joncs," and the name could be arrived at in a playful way by counting "un jonc, deux joncs," etc., until "dix joncs," or

11

Dijon, was reached, just as the French amused themselves by counting "para un," "para deux," until they came to "para dix," or "paradis." A Chalonnois was depicted as a "chat long et noir," and "Poictiers" might be shown by "ppp." "P" was pronounced "poi," and it occurs three times. That makes "Poi-tiers."

So great was the delight in the rebus that short poems were written by means of it. One of the most interesting is that of J. G. Alione, a "Rondeau d'amours composé par signification." It was published at Asti, in 1521, in a volume entitled *Opera Jocunda*. The poem consists of fifteen lines, all of which are represented in a manner similar to that of the following, which will serve as illustration:

PUIS   A   FRANC   COEUR   ET   L'OEUL

LA   CROY   POINT   TELLE

RE   MAIN   JE   DIX   PYE

SI   VINS   LANGUIR   POUR CELLE

A book written by Giovanibattista Palatino, and published in 1545, deals with the alphabets of different nations, and the various modes of expression. The rebus is represented by a poem of about the same length as the above rondeau. The execution is different, and there is a confession of weakness in the frequent use of letters. Still, it is curious, and it must have been a work of considerable labor. How far that labor was misapplied the reader may be able to judge from a specimen:

DOV'E   DEL   FERMO   PIE   QUEL   LA   SANT   ORMA

In the National Library, Paris, are two manuscripts, dating from about the end of the fifteenth century. The first is entitled *Rébus de Picardie enluminés*. In the sixteenth century two readers succeeded in solving about half of the examples. Fortunately there is a second manuscript containing 152 rebuses, which are, with only a few exceptions, copies of those in the first. In the second manuscript the solutions are given, from which it appears that the manuscript was rightly entitled *Rébus de Picardie*, since in the solutions frequent use is made of words peculiar to Picardy. The following represents a foolish woman with a bauble, *une mère folle*, a syringe which in Picardy was called *esquisse* or *équiche*, and a marigold, *souci*. The three words taken together—*folle, esquisse, souci*—stand for the sentence: *Fol est qui se soucie.*

In the two fifteenth-century manuscripts taken together, some 170 different rebuses occur.

Among the many secular and mundane interests associated with the Church, the rebus was one of those which found especial favor. When grotesque carvings in stone and on the misericord seats were permitted with such lavishness and fertility in subjects of a secular character, it is not surprising that the rebus should have been cultivated by ecclesiastics. It is a matter of ever-increasing wonder to the modern student of the Middle Ages how the Church encouraged, or at any rate tolerated, the secularization of what was associated with religious functions. An archbishop was prepared to play a childish game in the church to the music of the organ. Novices were set to secrete themselves in the triangular space above the flat wooden roof and shoot down on to the roof a load of stones, so that the worshippers might be terror-struck at the solemn portion of the service. The musical monks delighted in puzzle canons, which they wrote even in the form of a circle, so that it might be the more difficult to discover where the music was intended to begin.

So the rebus held sway, and its punning devices adorn even the pages of prayer books. In a book of hours, printed about 1500, occurs a prayer to the Virgin, of which the following is the first line:

The first image is a gold coin named *salut*, the second a bone, *os*, which is followed by *N.S.* Then comes Mary praying before a crucifix, *Marie priant Jésus en croix*. The whole line represents, therefore, the following: *Saluons Marie priant Jésus en croix*. Such devices in church and out served, no doubt, to attract the attention of those to whom reading was a difficult matter. It may have been partly out of consideration for the illiterate that some of the rebuses were invented. The illiterate man, it is true, would hardly be likely to find out a rebus unaided, but when once the imagery had been explained to him, it would afford him a ready and convenient means of recalling a name. Rebuses were, however, invented mainly because the invention was a pleasant exercise. In the English Church of St. Bartholomew the Great, Smithfield, under the window of Prior Bolton, is carved a bolt or arrow through a tun. This ending "ton" was frequently made use of in devising a rebus, as in Beckyngton (beacon in tun), Grafton (a tree rising out of a tun), and Singleton, to represent which name it was considered sufficient to draw a single tun. Abbot Islip's rebus in Westminster Abbey is a more ambitious invention, as his name may be read through in three ways: First, there is an image of an eye and a slip of the tree, then the figure in the tree may be supposed to say "I slip," and lastly the hand grasping a branch of the tree may be regarded as belonging to a person who is slipping. A piece of sculpture on the parish church at Ewerby, in Lincolnshire, representing a woman who is probably shaving a pig, has been taken to stand for Swineshead, swine shaved.

In France even the burying places afford numerous examples of the rebus. In the cemetery of the Franciscan friars at Dole was the following problem, which means *m, en dé, quat en dé*, that is, *Amendez vous, qu'attendez vous, la mort.*

At Langres in Champagne, in the monastery of Saint-Mammès, was once to be seen an epitaph of a chorister, on which were the notes *la, mi, la* placed between two death's-heads, the translation of the rebus being: *La mort l'a mis la mort*, or Death has placed him there, dead.

In heraldry the rebus was common. Prior Bolton, as previously stated, represented his name by a bolt through a tun. The name of Solly is represented in a crest by a fish, the motto "Deo soli" also containing a pun. The arms of the Laurence Oliphant familiy show two elephants employed as supporters. Corbet is indicated by a raven; Anguish by a snake with the motto *Latet anguis in herba*; Beckford by a heron with a fish in its beak; Tremayne by three hands; Papillon by butterflies; Martin by three martlets on the arms, and on the crest a marten cat; Roche by three roaches; Shuttleworth by three shuttles; and Manley by two rebuses, a man's head on the crest and a hand on the arms. Camden quaintly tells us of William Chaundler, Warden of New College in Oxford, who, "playing with his own name, so filled the Hall windows with candles and these words, *Fiat lux*, that he darkened the Hall: whereupon the Vidam of Chartres, when he was there, said, It should have been *Fiant tenebrae*." Of Sir Thomas Cavall, Camden wrote, "Whereas Cavall signifieth an Horse, he engraved a galloping horse in his seal, with this limping verse: *Thomae credite, cum cernitis ejus equum*."

It will be observed in these examples and in some of those which follow that the utmost license was permitted in the matter of language. If it was difficult to make a rebus in one language, recourse might be had to another. Anguish suggested the Latin *anguis*, Manley the French *main*, Cavall the French *cheval*, or, perhaps, the Latin *caballus*. There were French rebuses the solution of which revealed Latin words. Two mountains, *mons deux*; four bones, *quatre os*; and some monks, *des moines*, meant: *Mundus, caro, daemonia* (the world, the flesh, and the devil). And English schoolboys used to make merry over the play of sounds in the passage beginning *Is ab ille heres ago*, the interpretation being, of course, "I say, Billy, here's a go."

The story is told of a knight who invented a device to represent a temporary misfortune—a fall from his horse in a contest. To express the bitterness of his humiliation, when he reappeared he wore a burlesque costume, and carried on his head, instead of his usual device, a hard cheese, *Caso duro*, these Italian words also bearing the interpretation, "cruel misfortune."

Printers and artists have frequently made use of the rebus. The German artist Hans Schäuffelin is represented by a spade. The printer John Day took as his sign an image of the sun rising, with one boy rousing another from his slumber and pointing to the sun mounting above the horizon. The mark bears the appropriate motto

"Arise, for it is Day." A hare in a sheaf of rye, with the sun shining in the heavens, stands for Harrison—*Hare, rye, sun*. A rose inserted in a heart was the mark of Gilles Corrozet. Claude Chevallon was represented by *longs chevaux*, Pierre de Brodeux by *deux brocs*, De la Porte by a gate, and Jacques Maillet by a mallet.

The rebus may be formed not only by images, but also by letters, figures, notes of music, and by the placing of letters, syllables, and words, in such positions that the statement of relative position will supply a word or syllable necessary for the solution. For example, XL is written for "excel," EEEE for "ease," and I O U for "I owe you." Not so obvious is the series of letters G. A. C. O. B. I. A. L. in a French rebus, which means "j'ai assez obéi à elle."

A French schoolmistress is supposed to have sent the following report to the mother of one of her pupils:

> Vostre fillette en ses escrits
> Recherche trop ses aa;
> L met trop d'encre en son I
> L S trop ses UU ouverts.

Which is in full:

> Vostre fillette en ses escrits
> Recherche trop ses appétits;
> Elle met trop d'encre en son nid
> Et laisse trop ses huits ouverts.

An abbé, on being asked to resign, replied that it had taken him thirty years to learn the first two letters of the alphabet, A B (abbé), and that he wanted thirty years more to learn the next two, C D (céder).

Some of the rebuses formed by position are curious and ingenious. The most familiar are:

Stand	take	to	taking
I	you	throw	my

(I understand you undertake to overthrow my undertaking.)

And the telegraphic communication:

> Eight come nine
> (Come between eight and nine.)

In French are similar devices, as:

Pir	vent	venir
un	vient	d'un

(Un soupire vient souvent d'un souvenir.)

Trop	vent	bien
tils	sont	pris

(Trop subtils sont souvent bien surpris.)

But the most recherché of these is:

Si	pire
Vent	vent
J'ai	dont

(J'ai souvent souci, dont souvent soupire.)

In Latin,

Deus	gratiam	denegat
nus	nam	bis

means Deus *super*nus gratiam *super*nam denegat *super*bis.

An amusing example is where the repetition of *Jupi* three times justifies the addition of "ter"—Jupiter:

Missos
Jupi, Jupi, Jupi, as locabit tra.

(Jupiter *sub* missos *inter* astra locabit.)

The following rondeau contains examples of words to be understood by means of letters, numbers, and by position

la
BB DD qui est SX
las
Vueille muer dueil en
A xvi M.I. bieau sire di X
BB. DD.
Pour le servir de mi X. M. X.
M. OO dévots sans nul relas
BB. DD.

Of this the explanation is:

Jésus qui est la sus ès cieux
Vueille muer en soulas

A ses amis, biau sire dieux
Jésus.
Pour le servir de mieux en mieux
En mots dévots sans nul relas
Jésus.

A German example of the rebus in musical notation turns on the notes B-flat, B-sharp, and B-natural. In a book entitled *Frauenzimmer Gresprechspiele*, published in 1644, there is a somewhat extended rebus, in which use is made of notes, which are to be named after the manner invented by Guido d'Arezzo:

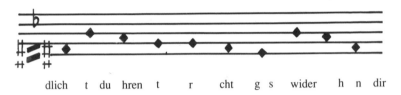

dlich   t   du hren   t   r   cht   g s   wider   h n dir

Redlich solt du fahren mit mir,
Recht guts sol widerfahren dir.

An ingenious rebus puzzle has been invented in which use is made of the representation of the squares of a chessboard. In each square is written a syllable, and the solution is to be sought by beginning in one of the corners, and finding the syllables one after another by means of the knight's move.

The rebus reached the height of popularity as a parlor game in the nineteenth century. Many family magazines featured challenging rebuses for adults and children, just as magazines and newspapers offer crossword puzzles today. In fact, the rebus as an entertaining pastime became a fashionable craze in Europe and America in the 1850s, 60s, and 70s, with book-length collections of the popular puzzle published in England, Germany, Holland, Italy, Spain, France, Hungary, and the United States. Since all entertainments of the day were intended both for pleasure and for "moral improvement," nineteenth-century rebuses, particularly in Victorian England and America, spelled out maxims, proverbs, biblical quotations, and even patriotic slogans.

Two examples, from the June 1870 edition of *The American*

Agriculturist, will illustrate both the moral sensibility of the Victorian rebus and the method of solution. The first is a very simple puzzle, the second more complicated since it depends on the position of objects illustrated. Both were provided with clues for the reader. The first is "a maxim, which, if followed by both old and young, would save much trouble." The second is "a very true saying ingeniously expressed."

By spelling out or translating the images word by word, number by number, or letter by letter in the first example, you will come up with TH, ink, bee, four U's, peak. Pronounce these words together out loud and you will have the simple solution: Think before you speak.

In the second example note that some letters appear *within* objects or letters, such as the letters "gin" in "G," which in turn is placed in the letter "P." Note that the word "the" within "C" is *above* or *on* the letter "S." In working rebuses your eye must catch the placement of elements—that is, whether they are above, below, within, over, under, or even in-between one another. Note, too, in many cases if an element is large or small or if a letter is capital (big) or lowercase (small). Think, too, of synonyms for size (wee, tiny, little), for synonyms play an important role in the solution of rebuses.

The second example, therefore, reads as follows: Ale, IFE, bee, gin in G in P, LEASE, ewer, and, N D in G in miser, YISO, F ten, thief, eight, OF THE in C on S, ID R eight. Read out loud together, the rebus elements spell out: A life beginning in pleasure and ending in misery is often the fate of the inconsiderate.

Enough examples have been given to show how largely the practice of rebus making has been followed in the past. As it is said that the worst puns are the best, so the rebus which is most excogitated is the most likely to produce a smile or a groan. The rebus is a light form of amusement in which the enjoyment consists in whimsical association and play on equivoques, where logic is thrown to the winds, and abstract thought aims at concrete imagery, which in many instances is curious and mystifying.

The rebuses in the pages that follow are culled from puzzles appearing in American magazines of the nineteenth century during the height of the rebus craze. They reflect the moral teachings of the day, of course, but they require a wide-ranging vocabulary, an ability to seek synonyms, a toleration of extraordinary puns, and, above all, a sense of challenge and an observant eye. Some of the rebuses included are simple exercises, but most are difficult and will set your teeth on edge. For the perplexed, the solutions appear at the back of the book.

PUZZLES

1. An excellent motto if you engage in fisticuffs on principle only. *Clue:* What is that collective group of people known as? And what is that person doing to the geese?

2. A bit of moral advice with a watery theme. *Clue:* Watch the position of the S's.

3. A quotation from Horace's *Epistles*, originally *"Dimidium facti qui coepit habet."* *Clue:* Note the incomplete last letter.

4. A truthful sentiment, but a difficult puzzle, requiring no little perseverance to find the answer. *Clue:* Watch the position of objects and letters.

5. A typical Victorian sermon, but still good advice today. *Clue:* A synonym may be needed for the first object on the second line.

6. This rebus was published in July 1865, a few months after the end of the Civil War, and relates triumphantly to the victors. *Clue:* That's not an ear of corn.

7. A very ancient proverb, sometimes attributed to Homer, and frequently quoted. *Clue:* Start at the middle, but don't forget the Ubangi.

8. A quotation from John Ray's *English Proverbs*, based on a line in Aristotle's *Rhetoric*. *Clue:* What's a three-letter synonym for "fence?"

9. A Victorian moral sentiment, as true today as it was in the past. *Clue:* Where's the signpost pointing?

10. Milton once called the subject of this rebus "knowledge in the making," but Shakespeare called it "but a fool." Civil libertarians would agree with Milton.

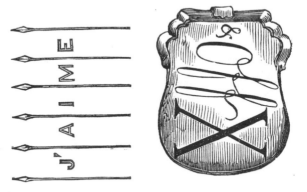

11. Two simple rebuses in elementary French. The first is somewhat sad; the second, good advice for businessmen. *Clue:* Watch the size of that ampersand.

12. Position and completeness are key to solving this simple puzzle, a bit of Victorian moral instruction and Sunday school advice if ever there was one.

B B and *than*
AND FOR *O*

13. Good advice, perhaps, but a very tricky rebus requiring you to describe the state, or condition, of some words and letters if you're to come up with a solution.

14. Probably the most frequently quoted proverb of them all, but phrased as the Victorians would have known it. *Clue:* What's that maritime object?

15. Good advice for the times, both yesterday's and today's. *Clue:* Look carefully at the two barrels, and note that what once came in chests now comes most frequently in bags.

16. One of the most beautiful passages of the New Testament (Luke 2:14).

17. Progress was the watchword of the nineteenth century, and this rebus reflects some roots of Victorian optimism. *Clue:* Watch that animal closely.

18. Another way of saying that appearances are not to be trusted. This is a simple puzzle, but remember that the Victorians loved monograms.

19. A political rebus from the last months of the Civil War, reflecting what the North hoped for. *Clue:* Watch that cake, and what are the two men doing?

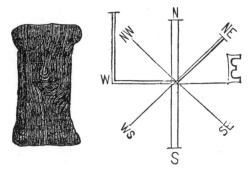

20. This is not as simple as it seems, but, if you must know, it represents a line from a favorite Victorian hymn.

21. The most central rule of all, and most excellent advice. *Clue:* You'll never believe the result of what that man is doing.

22. Here is a geographical rebus, which asks the question, "What four capital cities (one European, three American) are represented in the engravings?"

23. This rebus passage, in verse no less, appeared in the children's games section of a nineteenth-century magazine. *Clue:* What's an old word for wishbone?

24. This proverb was already ancient when Shakespeare used it. Rebuses don't come any simpler, though the second object *is* tricky.

25. A poetical quotation about the transience of human needs. *Clue:* What is the the name for a barrel containing 126 gallons?

26. Another Victorian sermonette, but Cervantes said it better when he observed that "patience is a plaister for all sores."

27. Here is a single word, which one should "endeavor to do plain." You should be able to identify it in five seconds or less.

28. Here's a bit of wordy, but obvious, advice that'll keep you guessing for some time. *Clue:* Position of elements and the squiggles before "Precept" should not be overlooked.

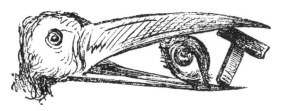

29. A single word, expressing what is most needed to solve the puzzle, even a rebus as simple as this.

30. If you've been solving these picture puzzles sequentially, you'll have come upon this old adage before. Here it is in a new pictorial guise.

31. Position is all in this statement of a very obvious truth about the difficult path to lasting love. *Clue:* Think of synonyms for the lovely woman.

32. Epictetus said it first, but the Victorians, with typical verbosity, turned his two words about forgiveness into eight or nine. *Clue.* The twig is supple.

33. A very familiar proverb. Just remember that *"à bon chat bon rat,"* or is that *"à mauvais chat mauvais rat?"*

34. Oft-given advice, sound even now. *Clue:* Another name for "bonnet?" One of many kinds of supernatural being?

35. A rebus of practical advice, made especially for the unmarried. *Clue:* Don't ignore the tiny object in hand.

36. A recommendation to those who stare at their feet in conversation, fairly obvious if you concentrate and think of Zebulon M. Pike and California.

37. Typical Victorian moral flummery, overblown and overripe, but pointed nonetheless. *Clue:* Separate the letters into phonetic groups, and the "B" isn't a misprint.

$J'ai$ 〰〰〰〰〰〰 $à$
\\\\\ vis $à$ vis du Roi

38. A rebus in easy French about a royal dinner. *Clue:* Start counting.

39. Our ancestors considered this a very serious question and probably had Eve and the apple in mind. *Clue:* What do you think our feathered friends are doing?

40. A relatively easy rebus. The advice proffered here is about as palatable to the young as the vegetable illustrated is favored by their palates.

41. A sentence of six words well worth remembering and suggesting that sufferance is a sovereign virtue. *Clue:* watch carefully and don't forget your subtraction.

42. A rebus for pig farmers. *Scorpio cymes*, a plant growing in the West and said to be harmful to swine, is the subject here.

43. "Cultivate simplicity," wrote the poet Coleridge, and this rebus is simplicity itself. *Clue:* What in place of water is being drawn?

44. A very obvious nautical truth. *Clue:* The sheep is a gelded male, and what about those punctuation marks?

45. It was said of Sarah, Duchess of Marlborough, that she never put dots over her C's, to save ink. This rebus is about thrift. *Clue:* Are some letters in the process of being written?

CRAAFAMY

46. One writer called the subject of this rebus "a state of mind and not an outward act." Benjamin Franklin deemed it "not hurtful because it is forbidden, but forbidden because it is hurtful." *Clue:* Watch positioning carefully.

47. A well-known truth poetically expressed. *Clue:* How's your Latin? *Nihil est ob omni Parte beatum* (Horace, *Odes*).

48. A picture puzzle illustrating an ancient proverb not entirely true in this day of ready-mades right off the rack. Originally of Breton origin.

OƒttƊe Ɗnn Š 🐓🐦

49. A moral sentiment about the hardening of the heart. *Clue:* Watch the double letters with caution.

50. Another Victorian sermonette, suitable for a framed motto worked in Berlin wool. An easy puzzle to solve if you know what the long-eared animal is doing.

51. Some challenging advice for landworkers. A subtle, but easy, rebus if you're good at synonyms and know your geography.

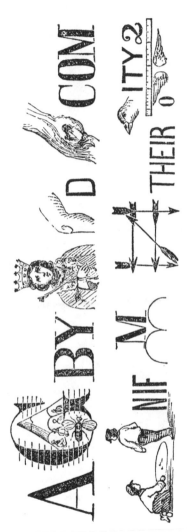

52. An American vision of monarchy, or, as Mark Twain put it in
Huckleberry Finn, "All kings is mostly rapscallions." *Clue:*
Study that complicated "G," and that last image is a
humdinger.

53. A dental truth painfully acknowledged, but a rebus trickier than you might think. *Clue:* Pronounce the elements out loud quickly.

54. The Victorians believed that "doing nothing is the way to being nothing," and they had a point. This picture puzzle, intended for the idle to remember, tells it all.

55. This rebus appeared in 1867, after one of the coldest Springs on record, and spells out an oft-repeated proverb.

56. "Duty" was one of the key words of the nineteenth century. Robert E. Lee called it "the sublimest word in our language." No wonder it appears in the Civil War rebus above. *Clue:* That's not a funnel at the end.

57. Two lines of a poem about the virtue of patience. A rebus incorporating some ingenious monograms, both alphabetic and numeric.

58. A well-known scriptural quotation, very nearly in the words of the text. This one may look simple, but it's tricky.

59. When this rebus was published in 1871, it was called "a self-ish man's motto." The "selfish man" was actually Benjamin Franklin, who wrote the words above in *The Way to Wealth*.

60. Victorian sentiment at its highest and most beautiful. *Clue:* In tonic sol-fa, what's a syllable representing a key note of a diatonic scale?

61. A quotation from Edward Young's *Night Thoughts*, and a truth worth considering. *Clue:* Try some imaginative synonyms for the first, third, and fourth elements.

62. Another moral comment about the acquisition of money, but probably still an acknowledged truth. *Clue.* Needed are the name of a sail element and that of a lady's accessory, c. 1865.

63. The Romans had a word for it and called it "Mala." How to face it is the subject of this rebus. *Clue:* Seek the word for a nautical guy line, and when is a branch not called a branch?

64. A nugget of wisdom is contained in a puzzle so simple that it should be solved in a matter of seconds.

65. This apostrophe to labor is a truth too often forgotten, even in these parlous times. *Clue:* The banging is loud.

66. Benjamin Franklin said this in *Poor Richard's Almanac*, but he lifted it from an ancient proverb first printed in 1578 in John Florio's *First Fruites*.

67. And here is a rhyming rebus about becoming healthy and wealthy and more.

68. Above is wisdom in rhyme, the idea of part of which is the first of the three maxims inscribed on the Temple of Apollo at Delphi.

69. Our elders believed that all doors open to courtesy, even if Samuel Johnson once called courtesy "fictitious benevolence." This 1865 rebus extols the practical virtue of good manners.

70. This high-minded rebus was intended for children in 1865 and was described as "very good advice, especially for those who are learning habits for life."

71. One of the most popular proverbs, which in its French form is *"Vouloir c'est pouvoir."*

72. A very common proverb, but a very, very tricky rebus. *Clue:* You and your eyesight play a substantial role in this clever word puzzle.

73. This fiendishly clever rebus won a competition for the design of word puzzles in 1866—and no wonder! Don't peek at the solution until you've given up hope.

74. An old adage, one used in part by E. M. Forster in his first novel, but still, alas, too sadly true.

75. This 1864 rebus was considered "worth reading by soldiers" during the Civil War. *Clue:* What is the second person doing and where is he doing it?

76. An immutable point, suitable for all. *Clue: Plus ça change, plus c'est la même chose.*

77. "More things belong to marriage than four bare legs in a bed," says an old proverb. Like rancor, for example? The rebus sentiment above is not new, but the puzzle is ingenious.

78. A rebus which gives encouragement to those who are working for competence. *Clue:* Size means everything.

79. Makes a statement which we don't believe a word of, even if Shakespeare did say it in Hamlet. *Clue:* A knowledge of old French measures will help.

80. This rebus asks a question: Where there's a will, there's a what? A single word is needed, and it isn't "way."

81. The Victorians likened evil to "a rolling stone" and took every step to halt its downward run by inculcating virtue and goodness. This 1867 rebus reflects American piousness at its most fulsome.

82. Temperance was rife in post-Civil War America, with one writer urging citizens to "beware the deadly fumes of that insane elation which rises from the cup of mad impiety." A sober warning's above.

83. And, after you've given up "the elixir of perpetual youth called alcohol," you can follow the pious advice above.

84. Few upright nineteenth-century men would have followed Tacitus's dictum that "in rashness is hope." This 1869 rebus offers a cautious insight for the rash.

85. A very good wish about the milk of human kindness. *Clue:* That's a letter of the alphabet around that three-letter word.

86. Denizens of Cleveland, Ohio, may like this one. *Clue:* Remember who the majority of itinerant goods pedlars in nineteenth-century America were.

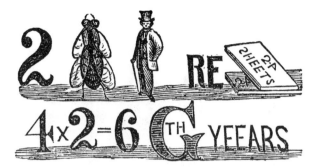

87. Advice to Victorian boys, and just as true today. *Clue:* Watch your spelling and the reverse-printed number of sheets of paper.

88. An 1865 Civil War rebus in support of the notion that battle is a drastic medicine for the human race. *Clue:* What's the state of the letter in the frying pan?

89. A rebus for July 4, 1865, the first Fourth of July after the defeat of the secessionist South.

90. A desirable accomplishment for anyone who looks ahead.
Clue: Start with the weird insect.

91. This rebus is a visual rephrasing, a new telling, of the Old
Testament proverb, "Drowsiness shall clothe a man with
rags."

92. A paraphrase in verse of one of the key elements of the Parable of the Prodigal Son.

93. An advertising rebus, published a month before Christmas, 1871, to encourage readers to subscribe to two American periodicals.

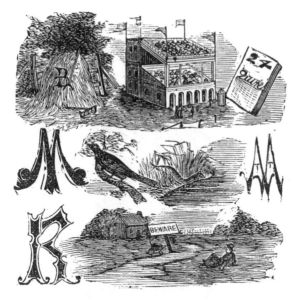

94. A more conventional way of saying that "one of these days is none of these days. " *Clue:* Know your paper measures.

95. An old proverb that rephrases an even older saying: "Spare the spigot and let out at the bunghole." Should take five seconds or less to solve.

96. A rebus for vintners in 1866. *Original clue:* Worth cultivating.

97. A frequent occurrence in American history, and a rebus not quite as easy as it looks.

98. A reflection of Victorian manners, once thought "good advice to talkers." Talk show hosts beware.

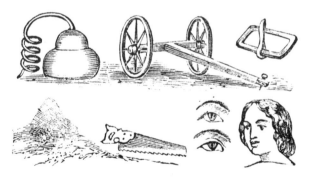

99. Another way of saying "Silence is golden." *Clue:* Read elements two and three collectively and beef up your vocabulary.

100. A circular rebus in rhymed couplets. *Clue:* The sheep in the first circle should really be a second pitcher, and what looks like the letter "O," isn't.

101. A simple five-word rebus, difficult in only the first three. *Clue:* Italy enters into this one.

102. A quotation from Shakespeare, infantilized.

103. A very common proverb on the theme of water erosion. *Clue:* Elements four through seven should be seen collectively as one word.

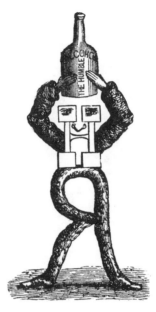

104. A picture puzzle about one of the central Victorian virtues. *Clue:* Watch that brand name.

105. A Civil War rebus echoing a sentiment famous in the political history of the United States. *Clue:* The second element requires a nifty synonym.

106. A statement about the formative years of life worth remembering. *Clue:* Position is all-important.

107. A verse from the biblical book of Proverbs. Unless you know your Scripture, this one may wear you out. *Clue:* Give the right character to the men shooting little birds.

108. Lines from a poem by Robert Burns. A very sad fact, and a very difficult puzzle.

109. Typically pious advice of the day in a simple rebus with a couple of challenges. *Clue:* The man's expression is key.

110. An old piece of advice about industry and sloth in a rhymed couplet from Benjamin Franklin's *Poor Richard's Almanac*.

111. This picture puzzle asks you to name an act of rude unpleasantness.

112. "Punctuality," wrote Oscar Wilde, "is the thief of time." For what his fellow Victorians thought, solve the rebus above.

113. More nineteenth-century words of wisdom. *Clue:* It helps to know what a governor of Algiers was once called.

114. A statement, even if overblown, that cannot be controverted.

115. An 1865 rebus tailor-made for red-blooded American boys.
Clue: The prancing critter is not a fairy or an angel.

77

116. Said on the death of George Washington by Colonel Henry (Light-Horse Harry) Lee on 19 December 1799.

117. A maxim perhaps difficult to make out in the illustration and not easy to exemplify. *Clue:* Look for hidden and disguised letters.

118. An ancient proverb about the teaching of children, rephrased by Alexander Pope in *Moral Essays*, and paraphrased above.

119. A rule for a successful Victorian life. *Clue:* What's a synonym for the noun "rip?"

120. Mark Twain called the subject of this rebus "the basest of all instincts, passions, vices—the most hateful."

121. An old proverb in a new dress, and very cleverly rendered.

122. A sermon for obstinate individuals. *Clue:* Once again, position is all.

123. For those who natter on. *Clue:* The final element pertains to caliber.

124. A poetical quotation from Thomas Middleton's *A Trick to Catch the Old One*, which, unfortunately for human nature, is all too true.

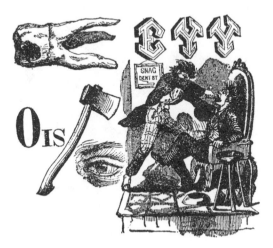

125. A true quotation, but somewhat toothy.

126. Equally true with the preceding. *Clue:* What did the boys in Company "B" eat?

127. You can solve this Shakespearean puzzle at one glance, but note the clever way it is rendered.

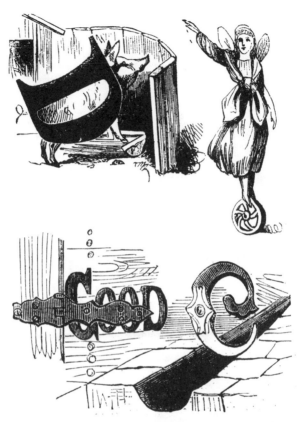

128. Uprighteousness is fostered in this ingeniously designed rebus. *Clue:* What's that around the Victorian toy's torso?

129. A political axiom not always practiced. *Clue:* The man is described by what he's doing, and ask yourself what the property of vinegar is.

130. An Old Testment proverb about idleness and the invertebrate class Insecta.

131. A descriptive name which has sometimes been given to the people of the United States.

132. Josh Billings likened the subject of this rebus to "Cologne water—to be smelled of, not swallowed."

133. A rebus about high purpose. *Clue:* The girl is a little sister and the man is slurping something.

134. One of many variations of a proverb for the sanguine that goes back as far as Aristotle.

135. A pre-Civil War rebus that reflects the institution of slavery in its rendering. The melancholy message was intended as a warning, not an example.

136. A rebus about two double-edged human attributes—and a true saying, whoever made it. *Clue:* Watch that monogram and know how to subtract.

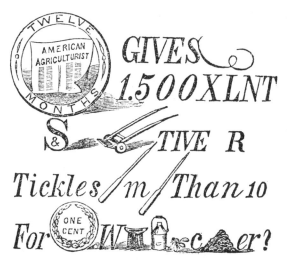

137. This advertising rebus appeared in the Christmas issue of an American magazine in 1864.

138. One version, cleverly limned, of a proverb that's been current for at least 500 years.

139. A true saying. *Clue:* Read this one aloud quickly to get the meaning.

140. In 1939 Bert Lahr embraced these words of wisdom. *Clue:* Try various canine synonyms.

141. Shades of President Carter's historic *Playboy* interview! *Clue:* Watch that caret in the last element.

142.   A maxim which is none the worse for being a rhymed one, although Spanish gypsies said it better and more imaginatively as "The dog that trots about finds a bone."

143. Identify the four cats in this children's rebus of 1872.

144. A double puzzle for the eye. When all it contains is discovered, there's a rebus to read, giving a word that has some fame in history. What is that word?

145. A rebus ingeniously made so as to read in *three* ways. *Clue:* Study the fancy letters carefully.

146. Victorian moral claptrap, but an entertaining rebus nonetheless and well worth the effort to solve it.

147. French for beginners, though what the Gallic rebus says is difficult to accomplish today without injuring the feet.

148. This one's a real challenge, though the phrasing of the double dose of Victorian morality contained within may unsettle the stomach.

149. Alexander Pope said it first in his *Essay on Man*.

150. A poem by Thomas Moore, popularly sung as the most sentimental of Victorian songs.

151. A trite saying worth remembering. *Clue:* The wing requires a synonym; the chains, an archaic surveying term.

152. A long rebus letter (above and opposite page) to young readers of an American magazine and from the editor himself. It appeared in the issue of November, 1865.

153. The commemoration of an historic event: General Ulysses S. Grant enters Richmond.

154. Much in little space. Once again, position is all.

155. A rebus riddle: How does the foot shown represent that its owner is determined to success?

I O 2 A A V & 000

O X 2 B & I X T Un 2 D

Now let 2+4=6 scholar ° &c

How T H E 7+2=9 I O un 2 the 3.

156. A rare mathematical rebus. *Clue:* A somewhat batty, but original, way to say upper-case "T"?

157. A difficult puzzle that requires considerable study to find the solution. *Clue.* Spot the nineteenth-century stereotype and review the clue for Rebus No. 86.

SOLUTIONS

1. Bee [as in a quilting bee], shoo-er, ewe R, rite before ewe-fight.

   Be sure you are right before you fight.

2. He, HOO, swim, S in S in will S, ink in S, OR, row.

   He who swims in sin will sink in sorrow.

3. Well, bee gun, eye [I], S half done.

   Well begun is half done.

4. S, tea, dig, A in S in small T, H in G, S in crease, wealth, mower THAN, watch in G and, weight in G, 4, sum, great T, H in G.

   Steady gains in small things increase wealth more than watching and waiting for some great thing.

5. Flies in WHEN, ewe, can, butt, face, IT IF, ewe, MUST.

   Fly sin when you can, but face it if you must.

6. Awl on R, tooth, E, boys in BLUE, hoof, AUT, and, 1 in F, reed, U, M's, caws.

   All honor to the boys in blue who fought and won in freedom's cause.

7. Many a slip between cup and lip.

8. Awl, R knot, THE, vest, hat, dogs, bar, cat.

   All are not thieves that dogs bark at.

9. All ways, bee, grate full, 4, THE, gifts, U, paws, S.

   Always be grateful for the gifts you possess.

105

10. O P in eye on IS, private, prop, ERTY, witch, THE, law, can, knot, C's.

Opinion is private property which the law cannot seize.

11. 1. J'aime in six lances. [I love in silence.]

2. Little and often fills the purse.

12. B under nose in 4, nose, laver, E, IS, half SO, pane, fool.

Be under no sin, for no slavery is half so painful.

13. Better B good, AND poor, THAN rich, AND good, FOR, nothing.

Better be good and poor than rich and good for nothing.

14. DO, knot, wreck on ewer, chickens, beef o'er THEY, R, hatched.

Do not recken your chickens before they are hatched.

15. Beak, wick, tool, urn, TH, eel, S, sun, switch, E, vents, tea, CH.

Be quick to learn the lessons which events teach.

16. Piece [Peace] on earth, good will toward men.

17. Type, and, steam engine, WERE, pie on ears of ass, tea on ISH, chain, GES.

Type and the steam engine were pioneers of astonishing changes.

18. You are not wise to judge a man by the coat he wears.

19. Rebel, lion, will, B over throne, AND, piece, RE, T urn, two cheer, OUR, country.

Rebellion will be overthrown and peace return to cheer our country.

20. I, wood knot, LIVE, all ways.

I would not live always.

21. Doe, toot, hers, a's, They's, hood, dot, OU.

Do to others as they should do to you.

22. Dublin [double inn], Concord, Augusta, Hartford.

23. WE'RE HERE on hand, two gather, BROUGHT on B, half of EVERY, one, RE, buss across stick, merry thought, CON, nun, drum, S, A, PUN, and, doll, THET, ricks in EVERY, stile, tomb, AKE, hour, little READERS, mile.

We're here on hand together brought,
On behalf of everyone
Rebus, acrostic, merry thought,
Conundrum, essay, pun,
And all the tricks in every style,
To make our little readers smile.

24. Awls, wealth, AT, ends, well.

All's well that ends well.

25. Man, W, ants, butt, little H, ear below nor, W, ants, T, hat, little L on G.

Man wants but little here below, Nor wants that little long.

26. Bear, miss, 4, tune, WITH, forty two D.

Bear misfortune with fortitude.

27. E, nun, C, eight.

Enunciate.

28. Line upon line, PRECEPT on PRECEPT, B 9 in junk, TIONs striking X ample, and Y's, AD, vice, R, knot in FREQUENT-LY over LOOKED, butt, X, P, RI, ants, N, four C's, A, less ON, awl.

Line upon line, precept upon precept, benign injunctions, striking example, and wise advice are not infrequently over-looked; but experience enforces a lesson on all.

29. A bill, eye, T.

Ability.

30. Many a slip between cup and lip.

31. IT, IS uphill, WORK uniting (joining) two hearts with a miss under standing between them.

It is uphill work uniting two hearts with a misunderstanding between them.

32. Bear, and, 4, bear, withe, long SUF, R, ring over COME, ewer, F, O's.

Bear and forbear; with long-suffering overcome your foes.

33. W, hen, THE, cats, A, weigh, T, he, mice, will, play.

When the cat's away the mice will play.

34. One's, hood, TR, eye, two, imp, ROV, one's, time.

One should try to improve one's time.

35. Matches, maid in hay star, of ten, ruin, US.

Matches made in haste are often ruinous.

36. Double U, hen, ewes, peak, 2, ape, R, sun, LOOK, HIM in the face.

   When you speak to a person look him in the face.

37. B backward in naught, butt, S, A, 2, TX [tex] HL [hell] in the EX, P, D, N, C [excel in the expediency], and F, IK, a C, O, fall, ewer under TA, kings.

   Be backward in naught, but essay to excel in the expediency and efficacy of all your undertakings.

38. J'ai, dix nez, à, cinq clous, vis à vis du Roi.

   J'ai dîné à St. Cloud vis a vis du Roi.

39. Hook, can, measure, awl, THE, miss, chief, ONCE in WILL, caws.

   Who can measure all the mischief one sin will cause?

40. Turnip, ray, ewe, 2, W, hare, Y's, men, WALK in safe, P, laces.

   Turn I pray you to where wise men walk in safe places.

41. Patient, S and purse, Eve, ear, ant, S will, pea E are [P.E.R.], form, one D, bears minus bee A [bears minus BA = ers].

   Patience and perseverance will perform wonders.

42. Cincinnati.

43. B, knot W, ear, eye in well, DO, wing.

   Be not weary in well doing.

44. Fowl, wether, stops, plane, sailing.

   Foul weather stops plain sailing.

45. S (penned), knot, W, hen, U M A's, pears, pear, not, W, hen, U M, A's (penned).

Spend not when you may spare, spare not when you may spend.

46. S in BR in G, SF in A, L RU in A, ND in F, AMY.

Sin brings final ruin and infamy.

47. In SOME [the word] Things, awl, in awl THINGS, nun, R, bee, LES tea [bee + LES + T = blest].

In some things all, in all things none, are blest.

48. Nine tailors make a man.

49. OF, T repeated, S in DE, D N's, C on S, hens.

Oft repeated sin deadens conscience.

50. F, ear, toe, doe, VILIFY, OU, wood, bee, bray, V.

Fear to do evil if you would be brave.

51. A, strait, fur, O, and, A, well, maid, fence, R's, ewer, signs, OF AN, XL, ant, farmer.

A straight furrow and a well-made fence are sure signs of an excellent farmer.

52. A, people in tent on bee in G ruled, BY, a king, knee, d, not, COM, play, NIF, M on arcs, arrow gate, THEIR, a bill, ITY, 2 over rule, O pinions.

A people intent on being ruled by a king need not complain if monarchs arrogate their ability to overrule opinions.

53. A, king, T's, hare, rill, ten ants.

Aching teeth are ill tenants.

54. Laziness begins in cobwebs and ends in chains.

55. One swallow does not make a summer.

56. He bears (or she bears), THE palm, thatch, ear, full Y follows DUTY.

He bears the palm that cheerfully follows duty.

57. Still, latch, EVE in GS, till, purse, ewe, wing, L, urn, tool, A, boar, & 2 8.

Still achieving, still pursuing,
Learn to labor and to wait.

58. 4, chair, I, T covers a multitude of S in S.

For charity covers a multitude of sins.

59. Keep, W, hat, WE GOT & GET, WAT, ewe, can.

Keep what you've got and get what you can.

60. Do, naught, leaves on G, two birds, AL one, NOR, bee, ewe, T, OF, sol, two flowers.

Do not leave song to birds alone, nor beauty of soul to flowers.

61. Shoemakers [awl men], TH in K, shoemakers [awl men], dead man [mortal], butt, hems, elves.

All men think all men mortal but themselves.

62. Tomb, A, knee, wealth, wood on LEAD, Eve-L [evil], button, leaf, ewe, reef, rain, FROM, mitts, purse, suit.

To many wealth would only add evil, but only few refrain from its pursuit.

63. Bear THIS in MIND, withe, stand, miss, fortune, and, miss, 4, tune, will, stay, knot, WITH, ewe.

Bear this in mind: withstand misfortune and misfortune will stay not with you.

64. NO, 1, 2, Y's, stool, urn.

No one too wise to learn.

65. C on tin, ewe, din, dust, rib, rings, C on tent, men, tea [T].

Continued industry brings contentment.

66. Cat, inn, gloves, cat, cheese, no mice [Note that there are no mice in the trap].

A cat in gloves catches no mice.

67. Cock, dot H, crow, TO LET U, NO, What, time, 2 rye S, FU, bee, Y's.

The cock doth crow to let you know
What time to rise if you be wise.

68. 2, NO, 1's, L, fan, doll, 1's, axe, COMMAND, D, note, sail, EDER, BORN, 2, rule, TH, eel, and.

To know one's self and all one's acts command,
Denotes a leader born to rule the land.

69. Ape, pole, light, address, GIVES, EZ, axe, S, two awls, O's, eye, ET.

A polite address gives easy access to all society.

70. BEZ in ewer, man, NER, sand, mile, din, words, butts, tea, rick, tin, MORALS.

Be easy in your manners and mild in words, but strict in morals.

71.   W hair, T hairs, a will, T hairs, A, weigh.

      Where there's a will, there's a way.

72.   On ST is the best poll I see.

      Honesty is the best policy.

73.   A band on a sinking ship, beef o'er the waves, clothes over her.

      Abandon a sinking ship before the waves close over her.

74.   Fools, rush, inn, W, hare, angels, fee, R, toot, RED.

      Fools rush in where angels fear to tread.

75.   Man, Y, a man turning a little pail before the cannon's mouth, eye, snow, a cow, ARD.

      Many a man turning a little pale before the cannon's mouth is now a coward.

76.   Awl weighs bee, PRE paired, 4, change.

      Always be prepared for change.

77.   Be above meddling in a family between man and wife.

78.   A little C on tea in U, a LE in CREASED, bee, Y, A, little ENDS in A, great D eel.

      A little, continually increased by a little, ends in a great deal.

79.   Tie S, now, tea [T], HE, witch in G, time OF, night, W, hen, churchyard, S, Y, aune [three feet, three inches equals the aune, an old French measure].

      'Tis now the witching time of night when churchyards yawn.

80. Where there's a will, there's a legatee [a leg at tea].

81. In D scribe, A, bell, X, T, C, B, long STEW, awl, WHO in THE, end [finis] over COME, Sin and, the FLESH, the world, and THE devil.

In describable ecstacy belongs to all who, in the end, overcome sin and the flesh, the world, and the devil.

82. Double U in E, ruins, many Sols.

Wine ruins many souls.

83. C on T in U in hole in S.

Continue in holiness.

84. Bees, ewer, ewer, rye, GHT, tea [T], hen, GO, a head.

Be sure you are right, then go ahead.

85. I long, 2 C, W, hat, ear, B tied on mountain, hill, and, plane, 4 Eve, R round THE, hole, world (wide), GOOD, will, 2, man, KIND, rain.

I long to see whate'er betide on mountain, hill, and plain, forever round the whole worldwide, good will to mankind reign.

86. Play in D, eel in G, eyes, a Jew, well.

Plain dealing is a jewel.

87. 2, bee, a man, RE, quires, sum, TH in G, ye(e)ars [more than years].

To be a man requires something more than years.

88. Warm A, ruin, thousands, AND, YET (in the end of 10), BAB less eye in G.

   War may ruin thousands, and yet in the end often be a blessing.

89. Lettuce, awl, key, pup in D, pen, dents, DAY, IN on R, OF, trees on S over THROW.

   Let us all keep up Independence Day in honor of treason's overthrow.

90. 2 bee four-handed in EVERY under TA king.

   To be forehanded in every undertaking.

91. B, WARE in DULGE, NOT over MUCH in SLEEP, 4, F, ear, pen, ewer, E over TAKE, U.

   Beware, indulge not overmuch in sleep for fear penury overtake you.

92. I'll go to tell Him all I've done,
   And fall before his face;
   Unworthy to be called a son,
   I'll seek a servant's place.

93. EV, rye, man and woman in North America, S, hood sub [under] scribe, four, tea [T] EH, earth, AND, home, AND, American, AG, rye, CUL, two, wrist.

   Every man and woman in North America should subscribe for the *Hearth and Home* and *American Agriculturist*.

94. B in hay, stand, ream [24 quires = approx. 1 ream], M, bird, eel, A's, R, dangerous.

   Be in haste, and remember delays are dangerous.

95. Waist, knot, want, knot.

Waste not, want not.

96. Eye on a grapevine.

Iona grapevine.

97. A, part E, OF, soldiers firing at THE end [of] D, ANS.

A party of soldiers firing at the Indians.

98. Bee, knot over urn, nest over LOUD, oar over shoe, R in ewer, T, awk.

Be not overearnest, overloud, or oversure in your talk.

99. A still, tongues, peak, saw, eyes, head.

A still tongue speaks a wise head.

100. A circle, OF, pick, T, ewers, ape, ears, inn, WHIC, hare, X H I, bit, ED, five pears, OF, ears. THO THEIR, 10, oar, ewe, can, knot, N, tire, LY, FOR, C, purse, sieve, ear, ants, eye, fan, C, will, give, ewe, the key.

A circle of pictures appears,
In which are exhibited five pairs of ears.
Though their tenor you cannot entirely foresee,
Perseverence, I fancy, will give you the key.

101. A roman nose, NOF, ear.

A Roman knows no fear.

102. A horse, a horse, MIKE in G dome, four, A H o'er sea.

A horse, a horse, my kingdom for a horsey.

116

103. C on ST, ant, drop in G, wares, a stone.

Constant dropping wears a stone.

104. H on R upholds THE HUMBLE spirit.

Honor upholds the humble spirit.

105. Union, muss, tea [T], AND, S hall, bee, mummy [preserved].

(The) Union must and shall be preserved.

106. FROM in fan, C, 2, A, doll, S, scents, A, man, SFUTE, ewer, POSISH on AND, stand in LIFE, R, U's, U, L, E, TAKEN.

From infancy to adolescence a man's future position and stand in life are usually taken.

107. Seest thou a man diligent in his business? He shall stand before kings; he shall not stand before mean men.

[In the rebus a man diligent in his business is represented as standing before kings, and again behind (not before) men shooting little birds. What meaner men than such are there?]

108. Manse in human eye, tea, tome, man, M, arches, scow, NT less thousands, morn.

Man's inhumanity to man makes countless thousands mourn.

109. Watch over ewer, hart, 2, key, pout, awl, vice.

Watch over your heart to keep out all vice.

110. Plow, deep, WHILE, slug, guards, sleep, and, U, will, HAVE, corn, two U's, and, 2, key, P.

Plow deep while sluggards sleep,
And you will have corn to use and to keep.

111. 2, bee, L bowed.

To be elbowed.

112. B backward in naught, butt, B, EVER on Time.

Be backward in naught, but be ever on time.

113. Fools on LY, C on 10, dey, GA in stay, 4, CET, hat, can, knot, B over COME.

Fools only contend against a force that cannot be overcome.

114. Awl in STINCT in D pendant, OF REAS on tea chest, hat, OUR, F, O's, R, toe, bee, AVOIDED.

All instinct independent of reason teaches that our foes are to be avoided.

115. Sum, boy in the U.S., BY in dust, tree, IS PRE, paring, hymn, elf, 4 TH E PRESIDENT C.

Some boy in the United States, by patient industry, is preparing himself for the presidency.

116. FIRST in WAR, firs, TIN, P's, first in the Harts Office, countrymen.

First in war, first in peace, and first in the hearts of his countrymen.

117. A man in tent on B in G over rule, D in awl, HIS, deeds, BY, prince, eye, PLE, ale on E, IS placed beyond the reach of FORTUNE.

A man intent on being overruled in all his deeds by principle alone is placed beyond the reach of fortune.

118. A S, twigs, R, bent trees, ARE inclined.

As twigs are bent, trees are inclined.

119. 2 in S, team, B on nest, man, lyre, VE, rent, and, love in G.

To win esteem, be honest, manly, reverent, and loving.

120. Key, P, MAL, ice in ewer, heart, and, U, harbor, A, viper, T, hare.

Reep malice in your heart and you harbor a viper there.

121. Better LATE than NEVER.

122. Two, bee over ten A's, CIOUS in TRIFLES in D, CATES A, LITTLE under stand in G.

To be overtenacious in trifles indicates little understanding.

123. A great awk, ER, IS, general, Y, a great bore.

A great talker is generally a great bore.

124. IF on [T] HE SUDDEN, HE, BEG in S, toe, R, eyes, gnome, ant, hat, L, IV's, can, cow, NT, H, eyes, NM, eyes.

If on the sudden he begins to rise, no man that lives can count his enemies.

125. Tooth, E, Y's, naught, IS, axe, eye, dental.

To the wise, naught is accidental.

126. Lyre, S, R, knot, 2, B, B leaved out, OF, RE specked, 2, THE, eye, R, AS, Eve, rations.

Liars are not to be believed out of respect to their asseverations.

127. Awls well, THAT ends WELL.

All's well that ends well.

128. D penned, knot upon Fortune, butt upon GOOD, C on duct.

Depend not upon fortune, but upon good conduct.

129. Hour, gnat eye on ale, RE, sour, CESAR, E, devil, OPED by ear, nest, CUL, chewer, OFT, HE, hearts, OF, peas.

Our natural resources are developed by earnest culture of the arts of peace.

130. Goat, tooth, E ant, tea [T], house, LUG, guard, C on cider, HER vase, and, B Y's.

Go to the ant thou sluggard, consider her ways and be wise.

131. A race of palefaces.

132. A-flat, TER, ring, lip, BRINGS, ruin.

A flattering lip brings ruin.

133. Two under stand, grate, D sign, "sis," A, marks, hoe, wing, soup, ear, eye, OR, cap, a city.

To understand great designs is a mark showing superior capacity.

134. One swallow makes not spring, nor one woodcock, winter.

135. Men, negro in seine over COME AND GIVEN over two D's, pear on B holding thief, ale, ewer, OF, long CHERISHED under TA, kings, butt, A GOOD, man, can, knot, bee, THUS over WHELMED.

Many grow insane, overcome, and given over to despair on beholding the failure of long cherished undertakings, but a good man cannot be thus overwhelmed.

120

136. Vice, S in fay, mouse, T, hoe, inn, ape, R in C, and VIRT [monogram], ewe on OR, A, bell, T, hoe in A, pheasant minus H [= peasant].

Vice is infamous though in a prince, and virtue honorable though in a peasant.

137. *The American Agriculturist,* in twelve months, gives over 1,500 excellent and instructive articles, or more than ten for one cent. What can be cheaper?

138. Ill NEWS, flies (held) fast.

Ill news flies fast.

139. A fool stung, M aches, miss, chief.

A fool's tongue makes mischief.

140. Key, pup, cur, age, tea [T], hoe, awl, bed, arc.

Keep up courage though all be dark.

141. Tooth ink on S in wreath, PLEAS, ewer, IS, necks, two ITS C omission [deleted C].

To think on sin with pleasure is next to its commission.

142. W, hoe, aim, S, BY in dust, tree, US, F, forts, tool, IV, May, M, ache, R, character, NO, one, can, G, IV.

Who aims by industrious efforts to live,
May make a character no one can give.

143. Catalogue, cat-o'-nine-tails, catacomb, catechism.

144. A cat may be found concealed over the bird's nest. The rebus is "Catacombs." The combs in the beehives, on the fowls, making the fence, and the currycomb on the ground fully supply the latter part of the word.

145. *1st Reading (across the whole of each line)*: Keep pushing, 'tis wiser to struggle and climb; to keep your eyes open; to conquer all fear; than be watching the seasons of tide and of time; of aid and of fortune; be steadfast to this; in life's earnest battle they only prevail, marching right onward, who will not say fail.

2nd Reading (halfway across each line): Keep pushing; 'tis wiser to keep your eyes open, than be watching the seasons of aid and of fortune, in life's earnest battle, marching right onward.

3rd Reading (commencing at the middle of each line and reading to the end): To struggle and climb, to conquer all fear of tide and time, be steadfast to this, they only prevail who will not say fail.

146. F, M, N, A, C, and, cow, R, dice, GO, hand in hand, WITH in DO, lance, and, LUX, ewer, E.

Effeminacy and cowardice go hand in hand with indolence and luxury.

147. J'ai traverse par I, SANS sou LIERS.

J'ai traverse Paris sans souliers. [I walked through Paris barefoot.]

148. Wood, U C K, lamb, eye, T, ass, O C, 8, withe, fools, butt, 2, S, cape, REP, roach, a band on VICIOUS, O's, I, E, T.

Would you see calamity, associate with fools; but to escape, abandon vicious society.

149. THE, prop, R, stud, E, OF, MAN, kine, DIS, man.

The proper study of mankind is man.

150. THE, last, rose, OF, sum, MER.

The Last Rose of Summer.

151. A, Y's, man, sum, time S, changes, H eyes [his], O, pinion, A, fool, N, eve, R.

A wise man sometimes changes his opinions, a fool never.

152. Deer, children, eye, hoe, pew, R, soap, lease, din, WORK, king over THE PUZZLE, column, thatch, ewe, will, bee, D lighted, two C's, O, long A, picture, letter, 4, ewe, 2, reed, THE AMERICAN AGRICULTURIST, D, sires, two inns, truck, TAN, dame, U's, and's, pear, snow, panes, two DO'S, O, sum, girls and boys, SEN, dancers, 2 EVRY PUZZLE, and, men E, mower, wood, bite, rye, ING, lettuce, C, HOW, well, ewe, can, reed, THIS.

Dear Children, I hope you are so pleased in working over the puzzle column that you will be delighted to see so long a picture letter for you to read. *The American Agriculturist* desires to instruct and amuse, and spares no pains to do so. Some girls and boys send answers to every puzzle, and many would be trying. Let us see how well you can read this.

153. Ape, reel, 3d, will, long B, RE guarded, a great DAY in the HISTORY OF THE UNITED STATES, and, OF, the world.

April 3rd will long be regarded a great day in the history of the United States and of the world.

154. Above, below, around, within, I wander in my dreams.

155. His soul is bent on it.

156. I owe to "A" a 5 and ciphers three;
Owe 10 to "B" and 90 unto "D";
Now let some scholar cipher up and see
How great the sum I owe unto the three.

157. A man in tent on chair eat tea above base, F, ear, disc on tent twixt [between] man and man, C's, naught, A, miss, N o'er C's, a Jew, DAS in A, kiss.

A man intent on charity,
Above base fear or discontent,
Twixt man and man sees naught amiss,
Nor sees a Judas in a kiss.

INDEX

INDEX
References are to puzzle number and not to page